N

N

A

A

Fabric Printing

LOTTI LAUTERBURG

FABRIC PRINTING

REINHOLD PUBLISHING CORPORATION, NEW YORK

Phototypeset in Great Britain by Filmset Limited, Crawley
and printed in the Netherlands by Joh Enschedé en Zonen, Haarlem
Bound in Great Britain by Dorstel Press Limited, Harlow

Preface

The dyeing and decoration of textiles is one of the oldest arts of mankind. The ancient civilisations of Mesopotamia and Egypt produced fascinating fabrics thousands of years ago, using only the simplest of techniques. Ever since that time, particularly among primitive peoples, very simple means have been used to produce beautiful results.

Even in these days of wide choice and variety in fabrics, many people know the pleasure of creating designs which are exclusively their own. Many others are searching for a creative activity they can enjoy in their leisure time, one that does not require a vast array of tools and materials. The simplest of patterns, the most elementary forms of circles, squares and triangles, can produce beautiful designs for fabrics; even people with no particular aptitude for drawing can find pleasure in making attractive patterns on material.

This book describes some of the simpler techniques of printing and dyeing. It also contains a large number of illustrations showing both contemporary and historical fabrics. These are not intended to be models for copying; but rather to encourage independent approaches in which the creator can find self-expression.

Contents

Acknowledgment

All the illustrations in this book show work carried out by the author, with the exception of figures 72 (Hildy Brunschwyler, Berne), 106-7 (Mary Dowse, Worthing), 121-39 (Museum für Völkerkunde, Basle) and 140-1 (Moritz Lüthi, Oberburg). The photographs were taken by Martin Hesse.

List of Illustrations

List of Suppliers

TOOLS

Lino-Tools, Knives, Stencil Brushes, Brushes, Sieves: All these are sold in most art and craft shops.

Tjanting-Tools: Some art and craft shops. Not easy to obtain in England or the United States.

MATERIALS

Cork: Any chemist or drug store.

Rubber: India-rubbers of various types from any stationer or art and craft shop.

Linoleum: Cut pieces of prepared linoleum from art and craft shops; linoleum in larger quantities from department or furniture stores.

Card and Cartridge Paper: Stationers or art and craft shops.

Fabrics for Printing: Dress-fabric and furnishing-fabric shops, and department stores.

Genuine and Synthetic Turpentine: Art and craft shops, ironmongers, hardware stores, and decorators' suppliers.

Beeswax: Any chemist or drug store.

Candlewax: Grocers, ironmongers and drug stores.

'Batik' Wax: Some craft shops.

Wire Gauze: Ironmongers and hardware stores.

PAINTS AND DYES

Poster Paint, Showcard Colour, Opaque Water Colours or Designers' Colours: Any artists' colourmen, art supply stores, or art and craft shops.

Fabric Printing Colours: Made by most artists' colourmen (colour manufacturers) and sold at most art supply art and craft shops (*oil paint* can be used if the above is not obtainable).

'Batik' Dyes: Craftools Inc., 396 Broadway, New York 13, N.Y.

Procion Dyes: Mayborn Products Limited, Dylon Works, Berryman's Lane, Sydenham, London, S.E.26.

Idigosol Dyes (Obtainable by special order in the U.S.A.): Dryad Handicrafts, St Nicholas Street, Leicester.

Bedafin Pigments (Not sent by post): Reeves & Sons, Limited, Lincoln Road, Enfield, Middlesex and Dryad Handicrafts.

Home Dyes: Chemists, drapers, ironmongers, drug and department stores.

1 *The Printing of Fabrics*

Fabric printing at home does not require a separate workroom or any very elaborate equipment. The main essential is a large well-lit table, covered with old newspapers to save continual cleaning of the surface. Tools should be kept neatly arranged to one side, thus leaving a clear working area, or laid out on an adjacent small table. The latter is preferable, as a completely clear table for printing saves a great deal of trouble. Care and cleanliness in working are essential. A plentiful supply of old newspapers to keep the table freshly covered, synthetic turpentine and plenty of old rags to keep hands and tools clean, can make the difference between success and failure. It is advisable to wear overalls or an apron to protect clothing, and anyone with sensitive skin may prefer to wear rubber gloves when using the synthetic turpentine.

Not everyone approaches craft-work in the same way. Some people bubble over with ideas, while others work tentatively and slowly, gradually developing their chosen ideas. Both ways have their place, but in either case it should be remembered that a very simple design, carefully done, will produce a more pleasing effect than an elaborate design executed without care. Time spent on designing, cutting and printing is never wasted.

In any craft the characteristics of the materials should show in the finished work. All materials have their own peculiarities: a cork block properly used has slightly broken contours and texture resulting from the porous nature of the cork itself; a rubber or lino block has clean, clear outlines. Thus, if smooth lines are wanted, rubber or lino blocks are best. If, on the other hand, a rough broken texture is required, a cork block would be preferable. There is no virtue in forcing one medium to imitate another. Hand-printed blocks of all kinds should be cut boldly and freely, without fussy or unnecessary detail, and should not strive to imitate machine methods. Naturally, all craft-workers tend to prefer one technique. There is always one which they find more satisfying and easier to do. It is, however, often rewarding to experiment with other ways of working.

Most of the examples illustrated in this book have been printed with fabric printing-inks or paints. These can be used for all the processes given, with the exception of 'batik' and 'tie and dye'. These colours are very similar to oil paints. One of their main advantages is that they are pigments, not dyes, and therefore need no elaborate fixing treatment. They are also cheap and easy to buy, as most art and craft shops stock one or more makes. They may be thinned or not, depending upon the technique to be used. They are also waterproof, so that fabrics decorated with them can be washed in luke-warm soapy water without spoiling the pattern. Last, but not least, they do not fade.

Tools should be carefully cleaned after use. This will be easier if done immediately, but, in any case, cleaning is essential as tools can easily be ruined if they are left dirty. All brushes and tools should first be cleaned with synthetic turpentine and old soft rags, then washed in warm soapy water, rinsed well and dried. This final washing is most important as brushes will rot if cleaned only with turpentine.

Fabrics printed with these colours usually take about twenty-four hours to dry; they should be either hung up or spread flat on a table. When thoroughly dry, and not before, they may be pressed with a hot iron, using a pressing-cloth or paper so that the iron does not directly touch the surface of the paint.

The enthusiast may later wish to experiment with other types of colour. Several firms supply pigment colours that have a synthetic resin binder, which gives a softer feel to the finished fabric. There are also some of the simpler dyes for printing which are not too difficult for the experienced worker to use. Detailed instructions for these are usually supplied by the manufacturer.

1 A well-arranged worktable

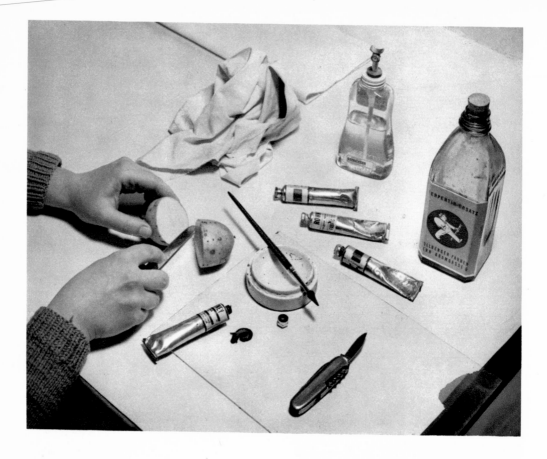

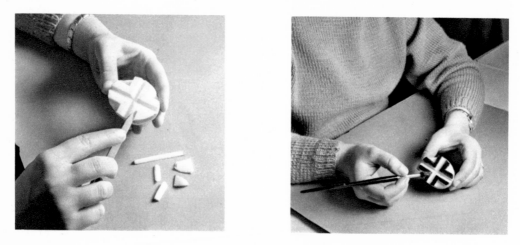

3-5 Materials and tools for printing with a potato block

6 Cutting the potato block

7 Colouring the block

8 Printing with the block

9 Paper-napkins with a variety of borders printed from potato blocks

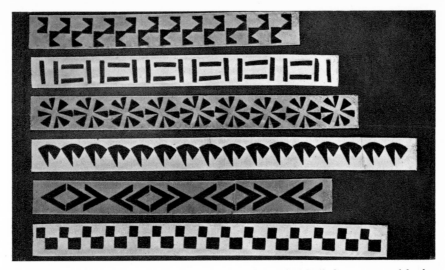

10 White, green and yellow silk ribbons, printed in black from potato blocks

11 Checked design made from half crosses and diamond shapes in white, green, red and black

12 Pattern of triangles from potato block; red print on light ground

13 Potato print in olive green and rust brown on unbleached cotton. The negative print is made from the oval shape of the potato with the outline of a tree cut into it. The positive print has the same outline cut in relief on another potato

14 Table-mat printed with potato blocks. The fabric is white cotton; the prints are in black, blue and red

Potatoes are not hard enough for very heavy pressure and therefore the fabric to be printed should be smooth, not coarse, in weave; suitable fabrics are smooth cotton, silk or rayon.

To mix the fabric printing-colour, a little should be squeezed on to the glass and thinned slightly by mixing with an old paint brush dipped in turpentine. The colour should then be carefully brushed over the design. The block should be pressed carefully on to the fabric, which should first be ironed flat and preferably pinned to the table to form a smooth taut surface. It is important to press the block carefully, without moving it at all. If the colour spreads it is too thin, but if the pattern does not print completely the paint is probably insufficiently thinned.

Potato blocks are often despised as a makeshift method suitable only for small children. This is not true. A simple block used with care and taste can produce beautiful patterns, but, as in all printing, care in cutting, in colour mixing, in the preparation of the fabric and in the placing of each motif are all necessary for a successful piece of work. The motif and the repeat should always be tested on paper or on odd pieces of material before embarking on a large project.

The more experienced worker may prefer to work in a slightly different way. Instead of using the brush technique, the paint may be spread in a thin layer on the glass by using a roller (which will be needed anyway for lino-block printing). If necessary the colour may be thinned a little with turpentine and if this evaporates too quickly more turpentine can be added. A fixative spray will spread it evenly and quickly over the glass. The block should then be pressed on the glass to charge it with colour. This is quicker than the brush method. A separate block is preferable for each colour in a design, though the same block can be carefully cleaned with turpentine and used for a second colour. It is, of course, possible to print with many colours, but, generally speaking, the beginner should limit these to not more than two. It is difficult at first to control large numbers of colours; and simple harmony or contrast is much more likely to be successful. Motifs should be complete in themselves and should not rely on elaborate joining and 'keying up'. A design with spaces between each motif is much more likely to give good results.

Almost everyone has collected a few old corks of various sizes. If not, they can be bought quite cheaply at any chemist's shop or drug store in sizes up to three inches in diameter. Smooth corks are the best for cutting blocks. Uncut corks print irregular circles with a crumbly, uneven texture and this texture is the essential quality of all cork blocks. As cork is a tough and brittle material it is suitable only for simple designs.

Rubber blocks are quite different. The material is soft, smooth, and very sharp-edged; precise, small patterns can be cut easily. Ordinary, used india-rubbers can make interesting simple designs, but for more elaborate cutting cheap new india-rubbers are best. Waste rubber can also be used, but this is more difficult to cut as it is usually much harder in texture. Both cork and rubber are more lasting than potato as they do not dry out or shrink.

Materials and Tools

1   Cork and rubber.

2   One or more sharp knives (a small pocket-knife is ideal).

3   An old paint brush.

4   A fine paint brush and black poster paint or India ink for outlining the pattern on the block before cutting.

5   Fabric paints and turpentine for thinning.

6   Cleaning rags and synthetic turpentine.

7   Paper for trial prints.

8   Fabric for printing.

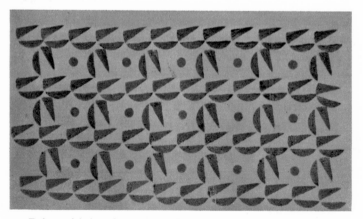

15   Print with bottle-cork; red and black on a white ground

To Make the Blocks

After the pattern has been painted on the cork or rubber with the black paint or ink, the cork or rubber surrounding this painted design should be carefully cut away. The knife should always be held so that the cutting edge slants away from the edge of the motif because, if this edge is undercut, the pattern can easily break away. Cutting rubber is not difficult but it is as well to practise on odd pieces to learn control of the medium. The amount cut away should be between an eighth and a quarter of an inch deep. If cut too shallow the colour may touch parts of the background and spoil the print, though this may be deliberately done to give a textured ground. With cork, the outlines must be cut first and the background very carefully cut away in small quantities. Practice is essential in cutting cork blocks.

16 Painting the pattern on the cork

17 Cutting a cork block

18 Cutting a rubber block

19 Printing with a rubber block

To Print the Blocks

Both showcard or poster colours (for printing on paper) and fabric-printing paint (for fabric) need to be slightly thinned. The paint is applied in the same way as that used for potato cuts. The correct consistency is important, but this depends on the texture of each individual block and the hardness of the printing surface. The material to be printed should be pinned taut over a pad. Several old newspapers spread out smoothly make a fairly good printing pad, but for more careful work a good surface is made by one layer of heavy carpet felt covered with a layer of plastic-covered cloth, both stretched tightly over the table and tacked down. Any fabric can be printed, but successful results are more likely with smooth, fine materials such as cambric, fine linen, silk or rayon. Very thin or very coarse, thick fabrics are less easy to use.

20 Cotton scarf printed with a rubber block

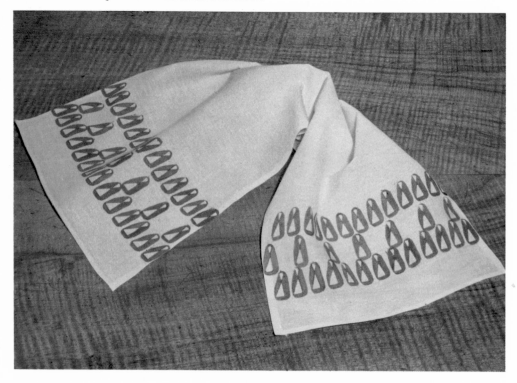

21 Wall-hanging printed with rubber blocks: yellow and black on unbleached cotton

The Arrangement of Motifs

Before embarking upon any large piece of work, the craftsman should know something of the problems of repeating the isolated block patterns or motifs in an interesting way. Blocks can be arranged in many ways: in vertical, horizontal or diagonal stripes, in isolated motifs widely scattered over the surface, in close rows side by side, the same block printed in alternating colours, and so on.

To begin, a small piece of fabric the right size for, say, a table-cloth, table-mat or scarf is a suitable and manageable size. It is safer to have the fabric larger than the finished size, at least an inch bigger all around so that there is enough for pinning, seams, hems, etc. For the very first print the easiest way to decide upon a good arrangement is to print a number of the isolated motifs on paper, to cut these out and to arrange them on a second piece of paper cut exactly the same size as the finished fabric will be. The cut motifs can be moved about freely until a pleasing design is made. Problems such as the arrangement of corner motifs can be fairly easily worked out on the paper. When finished, the motifs should be pasted down to the paper, which will be used as a pattern.

The material to be printed should be spread out and pinned smooth. The paper can then be placed over it and guide lines and dots marked through the paper onto the fabric with a sharp pencil. If the blocks are placed carefully to touch these guide dots, the finished design should be accurately placed. When two colours are used, all of one colour is printed first; the second colour is then over-printed.

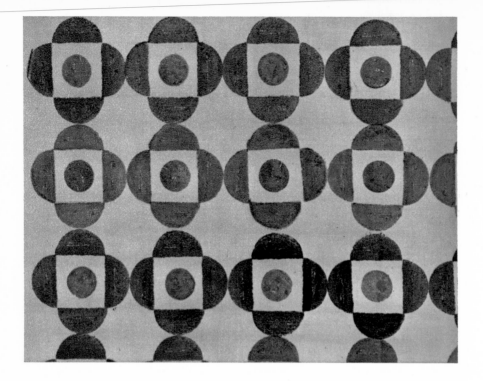

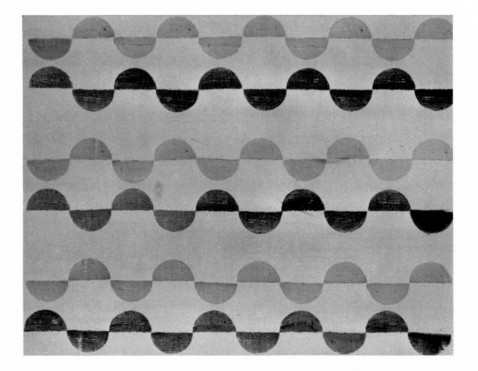

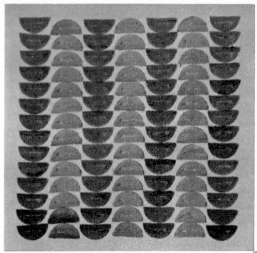

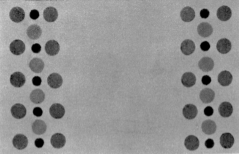

22-7 Prints from blocks
made with a whole and a half cork

28 Three-cornered white cotton cloth printed in violet

29 Mat in unbleached cotton printed in black and red with an india-rubber block

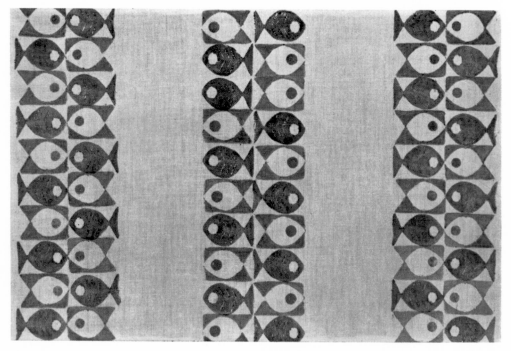

30 Lino blocks

LINO BLOCKS

Blocks made from linoleum are probably the most lasting of all, and the most satisfactory for larger designs. Linoleum itself is made from linseed oil and powdered cork on a firm base of woven jute or similar fibre. It can be easily cut and the finished block is firm and easy to use.

Designing for Lino Blocks

Simple motifs are the most successful for the beginner and geometric patterns are very suitable. The designer must remember that the aim is to produce a pleasing design on the fabric and that, although lino can be used to produce elaborate 'pictures' on paper, this is not suitable for a repeating pattern on material. Naturalistic landscapes and figures are not particularly pleasant when repeated many times on a fabric to be draped in folds, though a naturalistic drawing may well be the basis for an inspired design. The actual process of cutting makes simplification inevitable and the beginner should not try to force the medium to make over-elaborate and fussy designs. Children's work is often more interesting than that of the adult, partly because the adult often has so many preconceived ideas as to what a design should be.

33

The design should first be sketched, using either soft pencil or brush and paint. This should be done to the actual size, as this will save much time and trouble spent in enlargement or reduction. Designs should be simple and clear and without fussy detail. When the final design is decided upon, it should be transferred to strong tracing paper, using poster paint or India ink, so that it is clearly visible on both sides of the tracing.

Materials and Tools

The linoleum should be carefully chosen. It should be at least an eighth of an inch thick and as soft as possible. Plain or inlaid linoleum is satisfactory so long as there is no pattern painted on the surface. If it is too hard it should be warmed before cutting. Before transferring the design to the block, the surface should be given a coat of white poster paint so that the tracing can be clearly seen. This is more easily done if the lino is first well washed with soap and water to remove any greasiness.

Special cutting tools will also be needed. The best lino tools have the blade fixed permanently into the handle; these last indefinitely as they may be re-sharpened. They are expensive and one complete tool is needed for each type of

31 This drawing of an elephant by an eight-year-old is a fine example of bold stylisation

34

32 From a book on butterflies: such naturalistic representation can suggest general lines for design

33 Stylised, simplified representation of two butterflies

blade. The cheaper variety, consisting of a wooden handle with interchangeable blades or 'nibs', is quite adequate for general use. The essential blades are the knife blade shown in the holder (overleaf) or a small pocket-knife, two V-shaped gouges of varying widths (shown on the extreme right), and two U-shaped gouges (to the right of the holder). A small roller will also be needed (the gelatine roller shown in the illustration is very good but expensive; smaller, cheaper rollers can be bought in most craft shops). Also required are a glass slab; a spatula or old knife; oddments of paper and fabrics for experiment; turpentine for paint thinning; synthetic turpentine, and old rags and newspapers for cleaning.

35

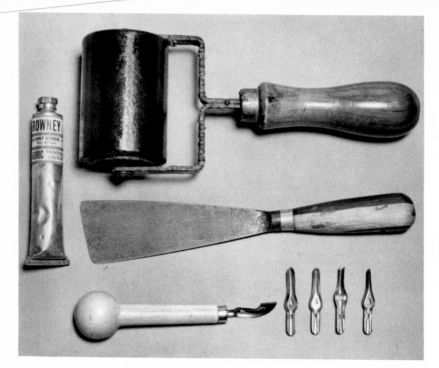

34 Tools for lino cutting

Transferring the Design

The block should be a little larger than the actual design or it will be difficult to manage. The India ink tracing should be transferred to the linoleum with carbon paper. The tracing must be reversed or the design will print the wrong way round. This may not be noticeable, but would be serious if, for instance, the pattern contained lettering. The carbon and tracing should be fixed firmly to the block with gummed paper and the lines traced over with a hard pencil. The paper and carbon are then removed and the pattern strengthened with pen or brush and India ink.

Cutting

The tools should be tried on a piece of waste linoleum. The knife is used for the preliminary cutting of outlines, the V-shaped blades for lines and small areas and the U-shaped blades for removing larger areas.

To practise cutting, begin with the V-shaped blade and try to cut lines by holding the handle firmly in the right hand and pushing the blade forward. The block must be held by the left hand and the tool must always be moved away from this hand as it is very easy to let it slip. Do not try to cut too deeply at first. The easiest shapes to cut away are lines, circles and triangles. Do not try them in relief. Positives, or patterns cut in relief, must not consist of very thin lines or they will break away. All edges should be cut with either knife or V-shaped tool so that the bottom part of the block design will be wider than the part to be printed; if the edges are undercut at all they will soon break away. When all the edges are cut, remove the background by scooping out the surface with the U-shaped tools, always working away from the design. It is better to remove this background gradually, in layers. If the background is not cut deeply enough it will pick up colour and print an irregular texture when the fabric is printed. If desired, this can be used deliberately to form an all-over background. Any rough edges on the finished design should be carefully trimmed with the knife blade. Finally, the block itself should be trimmed with the knife to neaten the edge.

36 Negative cut and positive cut

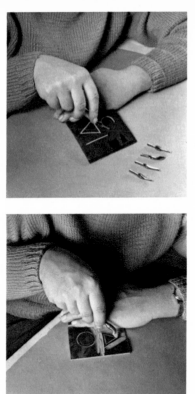

37 Cutting a line with a gouge

38 Cutting a corner

39 Cutting out the surface with a V-shaped blade

40 Cutting out with a U-shaped blade

Fabrics

Lino blocks print on almost any material, but smooth fabrics such as cotton, raw silk, fine linen, rayon, etc. are the easiest to use. Coarse or rough fabrics can be very effective but it is less easy to obtain a clear print. Very thin, soft fabrics such as chiffon should be printed with the minimum of paint, otherwise the finished print will be too stiff for the weight of the fabric.

41 Silk scarves of various colours printed in black with lino blocks

42

43

44

Printing

The design having first been tried on waste material or paper, a little colour should be spread on the glass slab and mixed with the spatula. This may be thinned with turpentine but should be quite thick and paste-like. The roller should be worked over it until the roller is evenly covered with paint. The roller is then moved backwards and forwards over the block several times until the whole surface of the block is also evenly covered. To test the pattern, a piece of thin paper is laid over the block and smoothed carefully with a paper knife or spoon handle. It is then carefully taken off, starting from one corner.

If the print is too weak, the paint is too dry or there is insufficient on the block; if the colour has blocked the spaces between the lines it is probably too thin. Any faults in the design can be corrected by recutting before printing. Material to be printed should be laid out smoothly over the padded table and firmly pinned. The block, charged with colour, is then pressed down firmly onto the surface. Hand pressure is not usually sufficient and the block should be tapped lightly with a wooden mallet or hammer. Larger blocks can be covered with a wooden board and smaller ones glued on to small blocks of wood about one or two inches thick. The blocks must not be moved once they have touched the fabric, and must be lifted away carefully after printing or the pattern will smudge. It is not easy to print twice in the same place if the first print is unsuccessful as it is very difficult to put the block down in exactly the same place.

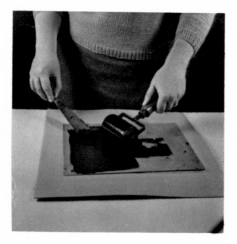

45 Rolling out the paint

46 Rolling the paint on to the block

47 Putting the paper into position

48 Withdrawing the printed paper

To get even colour throughout, the paint must be rolled carefully on to the block in the same way every time. The consistency of the paint is governed by the texture of the fabric. Very smooth fabrics need a slightly thick paint, but very rough, thick fabric textures require relatively thin paint. If only part of the design is wanted a piece of paper placed between block and fabric will prevent the paint touching the fabric.

49

44

50 Placing the block on the fabric

51 Hammering it down with a block of wood

52 Removing the block after printing the fabric

53 White curtain, with yellow and blue printed alongside one another

The Arrangement of the Pattern

The design should first be prepared on paper, then guide lines and dots put on the fabric as described in the section on designing for lino blocks.

54-5 Trying out a design by means of prints on paper

56 The final design, to be repeated to form a border

57 The completed scarf

Designs in More than One Colour

1   Alternating colours. Cut two blocks, one for each colour, and print next to each other, or use the same block for both colours by printing one colour first and leaving empty spaces for the second. The block is then cleaned and recharged to print the second colour.

2   Overprinting. First cut a block with predominantly plain surfaces; the shape should be very simple. Print this block in a light or bright colour. Then, when the paint is dry, print a second block over it in a darker colour.

58

59

60 Small cloths printed with lino blocks

Top: One-colour imprint
Centre: One colour overprinted upon another, blue on yellow
Bottom: Colours fitting into one another, black, red, blue

49

3   Fitted prints. These should be attempted only after some practice, as they are not easy and require great patience and care. A separate block must be used for each colour. Not more than three colours should be attempted at first as the use of more is very complicated.

Begin by making a precise three-colour drawing (61). Next, trace the outlines of the first colour very carefully on to the block (62a) and cut exactly according to the tracing (62b). Print this on paper (62c); then, lay the three-colour tracing over this print and correct the second colour if necessary.

Make the block for the second colour (63a, b) and print on transparent paper (63c), marking the edges of the block. Lay this on the first print and mark on the paper the position of the four outermost points of the first colour (64). Cut four triangles into the paper to fit these four points (65). Transfer these to the second block and cut the block away at these points (66). When this second block is printed the dots indicating the extreme points of the first colour can be seen through the triangular cuts of the second block. The third is made in exactly the same way.

61.

50

62 (a)

(b)

(c)

63 (a)

(b)

(c)

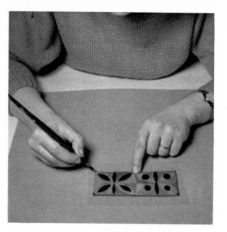

64

65

66

52

After Printing

The fabric should be hung up or laid flat to dry. When completely dry it should be ironed on the reverse side with a press cloth or paper between printed fabric and iron. The printed parts may feel hard and wooden, particularly if too much paint has been used. The 'handle' is improved after several washings, but dress fabrics must not be too stiff and must be printed with great care.

All tools should be cleaned and washed. Any left-over paint can be scraped off the glass and kept in an airtight tin. Roller and glass should be well cleaned with synthetic turpentine.

67 Lino block printed in grey-blue on white cotton

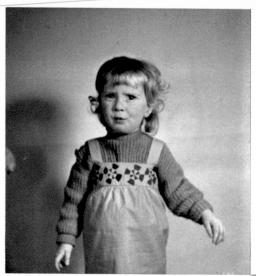

This and the following pages show the different uses to which fabrics printed with lino cuts can be put

68 Apron with printed border, in rust-red and blue

69 Cushion made of cream-coloured cotton, printed in red and brown

70 Red head-scarf printed in black

71 Wall-hanging made of cotton; black print on olive green

72 Wall-hanging of coarse linen with three printed figures

73 Blue cotton printed in black

74 Linen wall-hanging printed in yellow, orange, red, violet and black

Note

The experienced worker may wish to experiment with other types of colour. Synthetic pigment colours made especially for fabric printing are now sold in some craft shops. These have a rather softer handle than the ordinary fabric-printing paint and are not much more trouble to use. Some of the simpler fabric-printing dyes may also be bought. Directions for the use of both these types of colour are usually supplied by the firms making them.

75 Wall-hanging printed with lino block; black ornament on red ground

58

3 *The Use of Stencils*

As a form of handicraft, making stencils presents few difficulties. No blocks are needed, as the design is not printed on the fabric but applied directly with a brush through the holes of a pattern cut in cardboard or varnished paper. Very beautiful designs can be made in this way and most fabric printers will find this method a continuous source of inspiration, as the possibilities are endless.

Stencil cutting is a comparatively quick process and few limitations are imposed by the material. This freedom can be inspiring but can also prove a disadvantage, as patterns of almost any type can be cut and these may not always be suitable for designs on material. For this reason it is perhaps best to begin with the more rigid limitations of techniques such as block cutting and to progress later to the greater freedom of stencils. The experience gained in the cutting of blocks and the arrangement of the separate motifs prevents the over-exploitation of the looser and freer technique. Simple geometric and two-dimensional patterns are still preferable to elaborate 'pictures' and exaggeratedly three-dimensional designs. Unlike the previous methods given, stencilling is easy and very successful on both the coarsest and thinnest of materials.

Tools and Materials

1 Stencil board, cardboard or heavy wrapping paper to use for making the stencils. The wrapping paper should preferably be given a coat of varnish to strengthen it and to make it more lasting.
2 A stencil knife, small penknife or marquetry knife for cutting.
3 Heavy cardboard or glass to use as a cutting surface.
4 Stencil brushes of various sizes.
5 Fabric-printing paints and a palette or piece of glass for colour mixing.
6 Turpentine to thin the paint.
7 Synthetic turpentine, rags and old newspapers for cleaning.

Designs

Designs for stencilling should consist of clear, definite shapes; fine lines and small details are best avoided as they are difficult both to cut and to stencil.

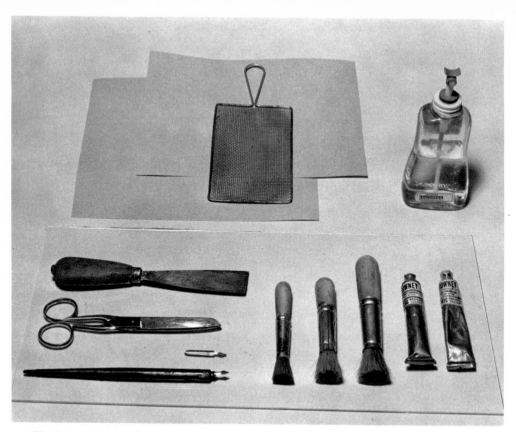

76 Tools and materials for stencil work

The design of a stencil must stay in one place when cut; for instance, although a circle is easy to cut, a ring must have two or more 'ties' at intervals or the centre piece will drop out. The easiest way to begin working out suitable designs is by folding paper and cutting symmetrical designs with scissors. These scissor-cuts can themselves make attractive stencil patterns. For any design in more than one colour each stencil should be worked out in the same way as that described for lino blocks at the end of the chapter on block printing.

The Production of Stencils

The design should be traced clearly on the stencil-board or varnished paper, leaving a border of at least two-and-a-half inches all round the design. This protects the background from accidental splashes while printing. The traced board

77 Painting the stencil pattern on to cardboard

78 Cutting out a pattern with a pair of scissors

79 Cutting out a pattern with a stencil knife

should be placed on a piece of heavy cardboard or glass and the lines carefully cut out with a knife. This must be very sharp and pointed and held like a pencil so that the tip does the cutting. Great pressure should not be needed as it is easy to keep a good clean line if the knife is really sharp. A small oilstone should be kept in readiness for sharpening as it is impossible to achieve a clean cut with a blunt knife. Simple stencils can be cut with scissors, but a knife gives much better results.

80-1 Three stencils used in carrying out the work shown below

Stencilling the Colour

When the stencil is cut it should be tried on a waste piece of fabric, pinned out as for printing. The paint should be mixed on the glass slab or palette and spread with a stencil brush. It should not need much thinning as it should be used rather dry and in very small quantities. The brush, loaded with colour, is dabbed through the stencil; the brush should be held upright to avoid blurring the edges of the design.

82 Dabbing on paint through the stencil for a simple pattern

When the stencil is removed the pattern should have clear, sharp outlines: if the paint is too thin this clarity may not be achieved. This way of stencilling gives a somewhat rough and granular surface which is characteristic of the method, though this will vary according to the brush, the thickness of colour, and the texture of the fabric. This slightly porous surface is effective but should not be overdone.

If a dense colour is required, it is preferable to build up the colour gradually by several applications, as one thick layer of paint gives an unpleasantly thick surface.

The stencil must be kept pressed firmly on the fabric and the edges carefully defined or the outlines will be messy and blurred.

Spraying with Colour

Spraying the colour is a slightly more elaborate method, but is very suitable for delicate materials, as the colour must be thin. It is particularly successful for larger designs and lends itself to bold effects and improvisations. It is easy to produce designs with one colour melting into another; blue running into red or into yellow. At its best this technique is capable of producing gay and light-hearted designs, though it can lead to over-elaborate and inartistic results if used without care and restraint. Taste is perhaps even more necessary than in block printing, as the method imposes so few limitations.

The spray method is slower than the simple brush technique as the fabric must be completely covered except for the design to be sprayed. The time spent can be cut down by making several identical stencils, fixing them in position and covering all the spaces between them with newspaper, so that the fabric will be exposed only in those places where the colour is to be applied. Although this means that a certain amount of time is spent in the preparation of the fabric, the spraying can then be done much more quickly and there is no risk of the colour accidentally staining the background.

In addition to the use of stencils, cut-out shapes and natural forms, such as leaves and flower petals, can be lightly fixed to the fabric and sprayed over, leaving a pale pattern on a coloured ground. Even very delicate shapes such as grasses can be used, making very fine and feathery patterns.

The only additional equipment needed is a spraying sieve or piece of wire gauze. The colour should be thinned with turpentine until it is quite liquid; the brush, moderately charged with colour, is rubbed slowly and regularly along the sieve, which should be held about eight inches above the fabric. This should result in a smooth, very finely-granulated surface of colour. Blots or coarse-

83 Spraying

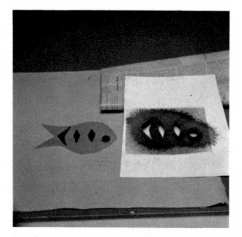

84 Sprayed fish design

85 Scarf, turquoise-colour silk lightly sprayed: grey more heavily sprayed; black

grained blobs mean either that the colour is too thin or that the sieve has been held too near the material. If the sieve is held higher, the colour will be lighter; a little experimenting with various thicknesses of paint and with the sieve held at varying heights will soon show how different effects can be achieved. The colour can also be sprayed on small areas by rubbing the stencil brush over an old comb or a scrubbing brush.

Using Two or More Colours

Graduations of one colour can easily produce a variety of tones. For instance, a single dabbing, applied very thinly, would give a light shade; a second dabbing over the first would give a middle tone, and a third a dark tone. The colour must not, however, be applied too thickly or the fabric will become hard.

Stencils may also be used without great difficulty for multi-coloured work. It is necessary to have a separate stencil for each colour, but as stencils are made quite quickly this does not limit the designer as much as the more rigid techniques; therefore a wealth of colour variations is possible without great effort.

The design must be very carefully traced and each individual colour cut with the same care. The lightest colour should be stencilled first and allowed to dry a little before the second is applied; when a stencil is placed over a very wet colour, it is difficult to avoid smudging. The backs of the stencils should be kept clean with a soft, dry rag to avoid any smudging from colour which has run under the edge or which has been picked up when the stencils overlap.

65

86 Place mats made of coarse yellow and white linen stencilled in black and blue

87 Cotton cloth, orange ground, stencilled in black

88

89

88-9 Stencilling the first colour (light), and then the second (dark)

90-1 A naturalistic drawing is the inspiration of the stylised leaf pattern on the apron border shown below; stencilled in two colours

90

91

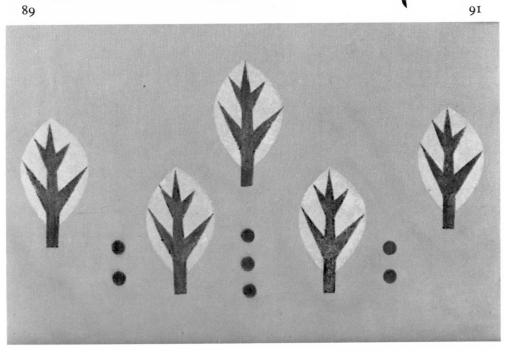

Removing Spots, Drying the Material, Cleaning Brushes

Despite care, it is very difficult to avoid accidental spots or splashes of colour on an otherwise clean surface. Accidental spots may often be removed by careful rubbing with a soft, clean rag dipped in cleaning fluid or turpentine. As this may result in an unsightly ring round the original spot it is always wiser to test first on an odd piece of similar material.

Stencilled fabrics often take considerable time to dry and should be left severely alone until thoroughly dried out. They may then be finished by ironing.

Brushes used for stencilling become very dirty and clogged with colour. It is essential that they be cleaned immediately after use by removing the paint with synthetic turpentine, washing in soapy water, and rinsing well before drying.

92 Flower pattern for a child's pinafore stencilled red, dark green and black on a bright green ground

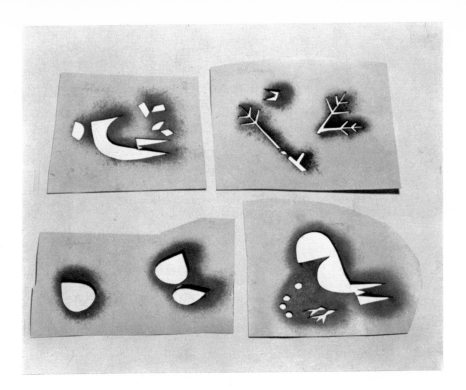

93-4 Four stencils for the pinafore pocket shown below; a separate stencil had to be made for each of the four colours, blue, black, green and red

95-6 Elephant on a little boy's red pinafore dabbed black, yellow and white

97 Mat and napkin-holder made of yellow washable plastic, stencilled red, blue and black

98 (*top*) Blue linen dress stencilled black
99 (*bottom*) Black woollen skirt stencilled yellow, red and blue

Screen Printing

Screen printing, which is used commercially for printing many types of fabrics, is a variation of stencilling. In its simplest form it consists of a stencil with a layer of gauze over the design, eliminating the need for ties.

A very simple screen can be made by stretching a piece of organdie tightly over an old picture frame and attaching with tacks or drawing pins. The design is traced on to the organdie, and the screen, except for the parts to be printed, is given a thin coat of varnish. This blocks out the background so that the colour cannot penetrate except through the pattern. The screen is placed on top of the fabric, held firmly, and fairly thin colour is then rubbed through, either by brush, a pad of rag, or a squeegee. The squeegee is most satisfactory; a simple one can be made from a firm piece of wood, about half-an-inch thick, three-quarters wide and short enough to fit into the frame of the screen. The colour is spread on one side of the screen and pulled across evenly one or more times by the narrow edges of the squeegee.

The screen must be cleaned immediately after use or the organdie will clog with colour and become useless.

100 Tablecloth made of natural-coloured raw silk, stencilled red, blue and yellow

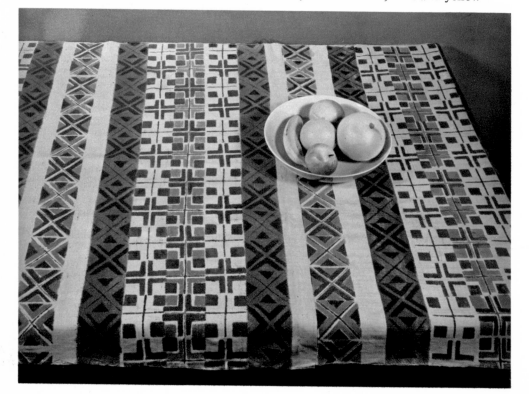

101 Wall-hanging, 'City at Night',
56 by 18 inches; dark violet ground
stencilled in various shades of yellow,
red, blue and black

102 Wall-hanging of dark blue material,
56 by 18 inches; stencilled black, white
and yellow

103 A German Santa Claus sack (equivalent to the English Christmas stocking), made of red and green felt dabbed black and white

104 Wall-hanging, 'Three Kings', 46 by 36 inches; blue-grey material, yellow, white, violet and red

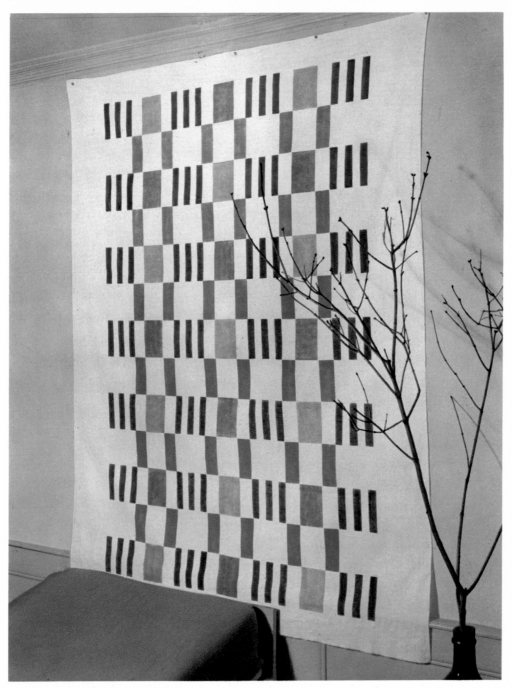

105 Wall-hanging made of white material, 60 by 80 inches; patterned in blue, red, yellow and black

4 *Colour*

Colour plays an essential part in the printing of fabrics. It can, perhaps, best be compared with melody in music. Without melody little would be left but disconnected sound. Without colour even the best-constructed pattern can be very dull indeed. Many people are blessed with an instinctive feeling for colour; but others have possibly never considered its many possibilities and may need help before embarking upon craft work. One can buy an almost infinite variety of colours in both paints and dyes, but a limited range is both more economical and much more exciting to use. Most great artists use a very limited palette, not from necessity but from choice.

There are certain essential colours, whether in paint or in dye, which, when mixed together, produce a good range of other colours.

1. A clear yellow, such as lemon yellow, with no reddish or greenish tint.
2. Two reds, a bluish-red (crimson lake, alizarin crimson, cerise, etc.) and a yellow-red (vermilion, scarlet).
3. Two blues, a greenish-blue (prussian blue) and a purplish-blue (ultramarine).
4. Black.
5. White for opaque colours. In dye the colour is made paler by diluting with water as in water-colour painting.
6. A vivid blue-green, such as viridian, is very useful for all varieties of peacock or turquoise shades. It is not absolutely essential but saves a great deal of trouble in mixing.

All these colours are very definite shades. They are needed because they are (with the exception of black) impossible to make by mixing other colours. Ideally it should be possible to find a red and a blue which are pure colour and which could be used to mix any orange, purple and green, but in practice this is almost impossible and therefore the two varieties are needed.

To give some idea of the possibilities of colour-mixing, equal quantities of the colours below, mixed together, make the following:

Yellow and vermilion	= bright orange
Yellow and crimson	= dull orange (the orange is duller because there is some blue in the red)
Yellow and prussian blue	= bright green
Yellow and ultramarine	= duller green (because there is some red in the blue)
Yellow and black	= dark dull green (black is made of all three primary colours, red, blue and yellow)
Crimson and ultramarine	= bright purple
Crimson and prussian blue	= dull purple (because there is some yellow in the blue)
Vermilion and ultramarine	= also dull purple (the yellow in the red affects the brilliance)
Vermilion and prussian blue	= almost brown (there is yellow in both these colours)
Vermilion and black	= a brownish colour
Crimson and black	= maroon
White and black	= grey

The less bright colours are not, of course, necessarily less beautiful than the more brilliant shades. The choice of colour is always a personal one, but it is a help to the beginner to try out deliberately as many different colour combinations as possible.

When mixing opaque paint or pigment colours, dark shades can be made lighter by adding white. For very light colours it is safer to begin with the white and add the colour gradually. A colour which is too bright may be toned down by adding small quantities of grey or black or by adding a little of its complementary colour.

Complementary colours are those which mixed together in pigment make dark grey, almost black. Red, blue and yellow are the three primary colours; when mixed together in the proper proportions they make black. The complementary of red is green, yellow and blue mixed together; likewise that of yellow is purple, red and blue combined; and that of blue is orange, red and yellow mixed together.

There is no such thing as an ugly colour. Colours only appear unpleasing in relation to each other. A strong red next to a glaring green is not necessarily ugly, but usually equal quantities of colour are less successful than, say, a large area of green with minute touches of red, or vice versa. Similarly, large areas of sombre colour can be considerably brightened by small touches of a brilliant colour. Numerous bright colours are not easy to handle, though a single bright colour next to a neutral or subdued tone is usually successful. Black or grey can be combined with almost all the brighter colours, while differing tints and shades of one colour can also be very beautiful.

All these details of colour mixing conform to certain rules. They should not, however, be taken as unbreakable laws and are meant only to help the beginner. The enthusiast will soon find that he or she may wish to break the rules and use colour in a more individual way. The only satisfactory way to learn about colour is to look at it and to use it. The would-be fabric printer must also remember that the type of fabric used will affect the colour. Red on a thick, rough cotton can look very unlike the same red on a shiny satin; on velvet it may look different again, while on thin chiffon or organdie it will appear paler because the fabric is so thin and transparent.

A note on mixing the actual pigments or dyes may be useful. Thick pigments, such as oil paints or fabric-printing colours, should be thoroughly mixed together with a spatula or blunt knife if an even colour is required. Separate colours in dyes should be thoroughly dissolved and well stirred or they also may be uneven. An uneven colour can be successful if deliberately used but if an even colour is wanted it must be absolutely even.

5 Tie and Dye Fabrics

'Tie and Dye' is one of the first ways in which mankind decorated fabrics and has been used all over the world from very early times. In its simplest form it is a very easy method of producing pattern on material and in more elaborate variations its possibilities are endless. The equipment needed is simple. All that is required is fabric to dye, a ball of string and a bowl of dye (ordinary home dyes are quite adequate for the beginner), together with some means of heating the dye-bath.

The fabric is either knotted or tied tightly with string so that, when it is put into the dye, the colour cannot penetrate the parts tied. When opened out this leaves a streaky white pattern on a coloured ground. Thin fabrics, such as fine cotton or silk, are easiest for the beginner as they take up the dye quickly, but heavier fabrics can also be used if they are left longer in the dye-bath. The dye-bath need not be large as the fabric is always tied into a fairly small compass and an average sized enamel washing bowl makes an ideal bath.

Tying

There are numerous ways of tying the material and the craft-worker will soon discover many of his or her own. Some of the simplest are given below:

1   Tie a tight knot in the fabric. This makes an irregular shadowy stripe.
2   Fold the fabric lengthways or across in pleats like a paper fan and tie tightly in a long tube. This makes long streaky stripes of colour.
3   Fold both lengthwise and across, then tie. This makes irregular checked patterns.
4   Fold a square of fabric like an envelope, corners to centres, several times and tie in one or two places (107).
5   Take a point of the fabric and begin tying, gradually taking in more fabric. This makes circles and rings (106).
6   Sketch a simple pattern on the material, stitch round the outlines with strong cotton, draw up tightly and wrap string round the drawn-up parts.

Dyeing

1 Dissolve the dye in a small quantity of boiling water and add to a bowl of cold or luke-warm water. Stir thoroughly.

2 Put in the tied fabric, bring slowly to the boil and simmer gently, half-an-hour to an hour for thin fabrics, one to three hours for thick fabrics.

3 Allow to cool slightly, take out the fabric and rinse well in cold water.

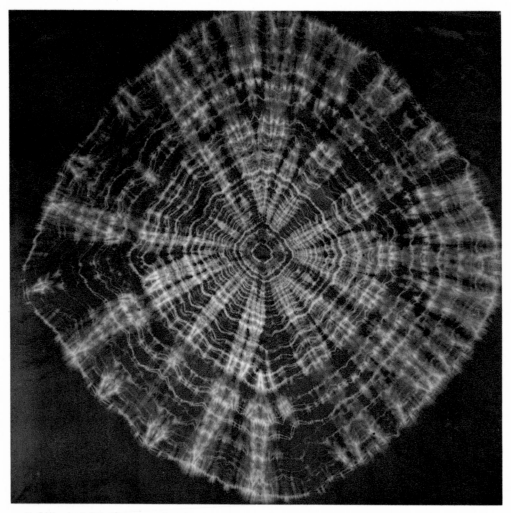

106 Silk tied from a central point

107 Silk folded like an envelope

4   Untie the string, using rubber gloves as there will still be surplus dye in the folds.

5   When the fabric is untied, rinse very well in cold water and iron till dry to get rid of any creases. If necessary the material may be washed in warm soap and water but should be rinsed in cold to 'set' the dye. For wool the water must be luke-warm and never quite cold.

Any make of dyes can be used and any fabric which will dye can be tied and dyed successfully. For synthetics it is important to choose a dye which is recommended for these fibres. The fabric can be dyed several times in different colours by re-tying various portions to give most elaborate multi-coloured effects. It must, however, be remembered that, as dye is quite transparent, it is impossible to dye a fabric lighter than its original colour.

6 Batik Work

Batik is the Javanese name for one of the oldest and most wide-spread ways of decorating fabrics known to mankind. The Javanese batiks have become so famous that the name is now commonly used for all fabrics decorated in this way wherever they have been made. Briefly, the pattern on these materials is made by painting the whole design on the fabric with very hot liquid wax before immersing the whole in a dye-bath. The wax prevents the dye reaching the painted pattern and the finished material is left with a pale pattern on a coloured ground. The wax is sometimes deliberately cracked to form fine spider-like lines of colour where the dye penetrates these cracks. The dye-bath is, of course, always cold, as otherwise the wax would melt and the pattern be spoilt. This is a fascinating and exciting craft, well within the scope of anyone with an interest in making beautiful fabrics.

Javanese batiks are often very elaborate, using many colours in delicate patterns with names like 'Butterflies in flight' and 'Summer clouds in the sky'; but the simplest patterns are often just as beautiful and there is no need for complicated techniques in order to make very attractive fabrics. As these fabrics are all coloured with dye they can be used successfully where light is to shine through them, for instance for lampshades, as the colour is transparent.

Designs for batik need a free and adventurous approach. A careful pencil drawing is not easy to translate into terms of wax and dye; the easiest way to try out ideas is to use coloured paper as a ground and pale opaque paint to make the pattern. Better still, the design can be drawn with wax crayon and coloured ink washed over the whole paper. The wax crayon will prevent the colour staining the paper and leave a pale pattern on coloured ground just as the painted wax prevents the dye staining the fabric.

Fabrics, Materials and Tools

Thin, smooth fabrics are the easiest to use and are essential for small, delicate patterns. Most Javanese fabrics are on fine cotton, similar to lawn, or on thin silk like Japanese silk. Silk is perhaps the easiest fabric of all to use, with fine lawns

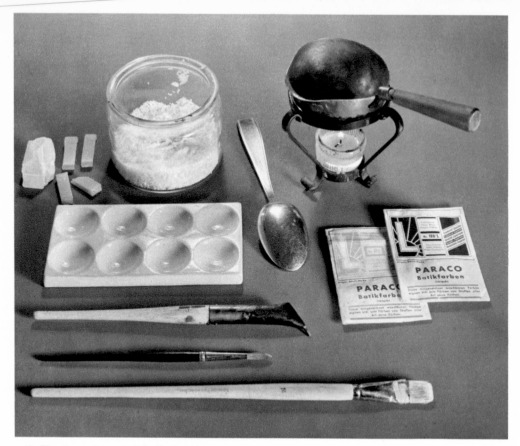

108 Tools and materials for batik

a close second. Organdie, voile, chiffon, georgette and very fine wool voiles are also easy. Synthetic fabrics are not easy to dye, and drip-dry finishes may also be difficult. Heavy, coarse and thick fabrics are not much used, though large-scale simple patterns on these can be very effective; they are, however, more difficult to handle. All fabrics should be thoroughly washed and ironed before use and cottons should be boiled in fairly strong soap or detergent to remove any dressing. Dyes will not 'take' properly if the fabric is not clean.

Beeswax is the best wax to use for fine lines or small areas. This is rather expensive but is more manageable and cracks less than other kinds. For large areas a wax made of equal quantities of beeswax and paraffin wax is suitable. Old pieces of candle and beeswax make a good mixture. Some firms make a special 'Batik wax' ready mixed. Too much beeswax makes the mixture sticky and difficult to remove, while too much of any other wax cracks off easily and spoils the clarity of the design. Cold weather will make the wax more brittle and hot weather will make it less so.

Brushes of various sizes will also be needed to apply the wax. If neglected these will wear out rather quickly, but their life will be considerably lengthened if the wax is rinsed out in petrol (gasoline) or benzine immediately after use. They should then be washed in warm water and soap and thoroughly rinsed and dried. Cheap brushes can be used for large areas but one or two good sable brushes should be kept for fine lines, as the cheaper brushes are too soft and difficult to control. The Javanese use a 'tjanting' tool to apply the wax. This consists of a handle fitted to a small cup with a spout. These are, however, not always easy to obtain and good brushes are quite adequate for the beginner.

Dyes will be needed for colouring the fabric. There are several types of dye which can be used cold, but many of them are not suitable for the beginner. The easiest to use are those made especially for batik. These are very simple to use and give quite good results with reasonable care. They are made by firms specializing in craft materials.

One or more large bowls will be needed for use as dye-baths as well as several small basins or mugs for dye-mixing. These can be of glass, china, plastic or enamel, but not of metal as metal salts are used in many dyeing processes and metal vessels may alter the colour of the dyes.

Before the painting of the design can begin, the fabric must be stretched firmly over a frame (an old picture frame will do) and attached with drawing pins so that the cloth is quite taut. The designs can be sketched lightly on the fabric with a sharp pencil before applying the wax.

As wax is inflammable it should never be heated directly over a flame but should be placed in a small tin or enamel mug in a saucepan of boiling water. The water should reach well up the sides of the tin so that the wax melts quickly but not so high that the boiling water spills into the wax. The saucepan should be kept boiling until the wax is so hot and thin that it soaks through the fabric the moment it is painted on. The pan can then be removed from the heat; the water will keep the wax hot for a considerable time.

Brushes are dipped straight into the wax but the tjanting tool must be heated and filled with melted wax. For the simplest batik, the design is painted on the material with wax and the whole immersed in cold water before dying to ensure that the wax is quite hard and set. The dye powder is mixed with a little hot water so that it is thoroughly dissolved and this concentrated liquid is added to a bowl of cold water. The bowl must be large enough and contain enough water for the fabric to float freely in the dye. If the dye-bath is too small the colour will not be even. The amount of dye powder depends upon the kind of dye and on the strength of colour required; directions are usually given with each firm's individual dye-stuffs. The colour may be tested by immersing small pieces of the fabric in the dye-bath before dyeing the final piece. These test pieces should be dried as the colour always looks much darker when wet.

When the dye-bath is ready, the waxed material is taken out of the cold water and squeezed well to crack the wax, if necessary, before placing it in the bath of dye. It should be turned gently once or twice to ensure even dyeing and left in the dye for between fifteen and thirty minutes. It is then taken out and hung up by the corners to dry. It should not be hung over a line as this stains the line itself and may make a line of uneven dye across the fold of fabric.

When dry, the wax must be removed. Any very thick wax can be cracked off by working the fabric with the hands, and the remainder can be ironed out by placing several sheets of newspaper or tissue paper above and below the fabric and ironing it with a hot iron. The paper must be frequently replaced as it absorbs the wax and becomes useless. Finally the fabric is 'washed' in benzine or petrol (gasoline). Because both these liquids are very inflammable, this should be done in the open air, well away from any heat or flames. Allow the fabric to hang up long enough for the fumes to evaporate; then iron the fabric to give a smooth finish.

This method produces a fabric with a light pattern on a coloured ground. If more colours are wanted the outlines of the design are first painted with wax, completely surrounding each separate colour area. The colour is then painted with the concentrated liquid dye. When completely dry all the coloured areas are covered with wax. The whole fabric is then immersed in the dye-bath for the ground colour and finished as before, making a multi-coloured design on a coloured background.

Some of the most interesting batik fabrics are made by a slightly more complicated method, though this is not really difficult and gives more permanent results. First of all, the parts of the design to be left white are waxed and the fabric dyed a pale colour, say yellow. The fabric is dried and the parts to be left yellow are waxed before dyeing the whole blue. This will give a pattern in white and yellow on a greenish-blue background. This is a very simple example, but

109 Drawing the pattern on the fabric

110 Filling the tjanting tool with wax

111 Heating it over a candle-flame

it is possible to use varying colours and depths of colour to make very elaborate pattern and colour schemes. An important point to remember is that each colour will affect the next colour used over it.

True Javanese batik is often made by an even more complicated method, though even this is not really difficult. To make a multi-coloured fabric, the whole surface is waxed except for those parts to be blue or green. It is dyed blue, dried and the wax removed. The whole fabric is then covered with wax except for the parts to be red and is again dyed, dried and washed. Next, the parts to be yellow and green are left unwaxed and it is dyed in a yellow bath; the parts to be green have already been dyed blue and blue and yellow combined make green. The background is often left unwaxed throughout so that all the dyes affect it and a very dark background colour is made.

Batik fabrics can be dyed with 'batik' dyes. It is also possible to use ordinary home dyes, though these must be used cold and it is therefore difficult to obtain very dark shades. Batik need not be confined to fabric alone. The same technique can be used on paper and this is a cheaper way not only of carrying out ideas for fabrics but also of producing interesting patterned papers for a variety of uses. It can also be used to decorate wood, with wood stains as 'dyes', and the enthusiast will no doubt discover many other variations of this technique.

112 Applying the wax

113 Painting with different colours

90

114 Covering the colours with wax

115 Squeezing the fabric to crack the wax

116 Dyeing

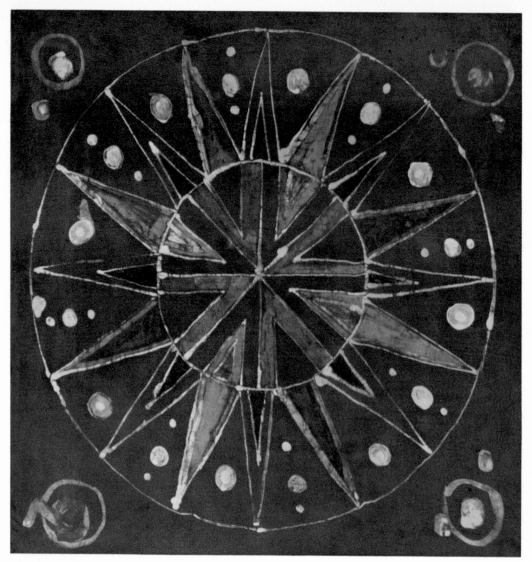

117 Red-dyed batik cloth

92

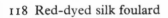
118 Red-dyed silk foulard

119 Scarf dyed and painted yellow, green and red

120 Piece of batik work which can be used as a wall-hanging,
painted brown and red and dyed green in the dye-bath

7 *Historical Examples*

The pages which follow show printed and dyed materials of various places and times. They are illustrated here to encourage the student to produce original work; for they were inspired by the same desire as ours, to beautify our lives by simple means.

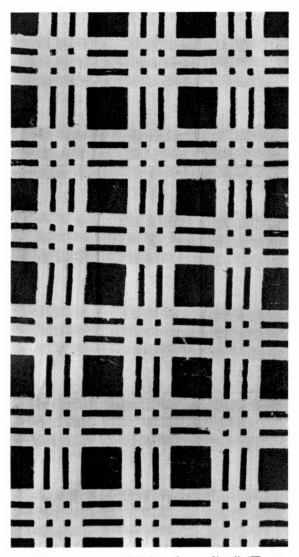

121 Japanese cotton fabric; a form of batik (Tenn-Gui); red-brown on a white ground

122 Japanese batik cloth with a dark blue ground, multi-coloured pattern

123 Chinese Turkestan. Cotton fabric with a 'plangi' or tie-and-dye pattern. The circular patterns are formed by drawing together and tying the material with thread or bast before dyeing; brick red ground, the circular pattern, yellow, red, violet and white; size 16 by 24 inches

124 Chinese batik on cotton material; cushion-cover for an infant's carrying-cloth

125 Batik cloth from Java representing puppets; black, brownish-ochre, blue and white

126 Section of a Javanese head-scarf in batik work; size of scarf 40 inches square; white ground with red and blue design

127 Historic textile from Peru (11th-12th century A.D.); painted wool with dark brown pattern on white ground

128 Batik-like cotton fabric from Africa; blue on a white ground

129 A variety of block-painted patterns from the Gold Coast. The blocks were produced according to old traditional patterns from pumpkin rind and similar material.
These patterns partly represent proverbs: the two crossed crocodiles (top right), for
instance, signify 'Two heads, two necks, but only one belly', meaning family unity and
loyalty. White printed in dark brown

130-4 On the right and on the two pages following are enlarged illustrations of the same
material, excellent examples of bold stylisation

131

132

133

134

135 Cotton batik from Nigeria; blue on a white ground

136 Man's tunic from Sudan; cotton material with batik treatment, dyed black

137 Section of an Indian temple-hanging: pattern built out of human and animal figures imposed by printing (probably with a wooden block) on white cotton

138 Reverse patterned fabric from Nigeria; blue on a white ground. This is a similar process to batik but some resist other than wax, such as leaves or bark, had been sewn to the parts that were to be left uncoloured

139 Hand print with wooden blocks from the canton of Grisons in Switzerland; red and black

140 Printed flour sack
from Switzerland (1888)

141 Family coats-of-arms used on blocks for printing flour sacks